DOGS THROUGHOUT HISTORY™

The Story of the Boxer

Martha Mulvany

The Rosen Publishing Group's
PowerKids Press™
New York

For bad dogs everywhere, especially Guido and Pipo.

Published in 2000 by The Rosen Publishing Group, Inc.
29 East 21st Street, New York, NY 10010

Copyright © 2000 by The Rosen Publishing Group, Inc.

First Edition

Book design: Danielle Primiceri

Photo credits: Cover © Fritz Prenzel/Animals Animals; p. 4 © Barbara Wright/Animals Animals; p. 7 © CORBIS/Anthony Bannister; ABPL; p. 8 © CORBIS/Hulton-Deutsch Collection; pp. 11, 12 © Superstock, Inc; p. 15 © Robert Pearcy/Animals Animals; pp. 16, 19 © Hulton Getty/Liaison Agency; p. 20 © CORBIS/Paul Almasy.

Mulvany, Martha, 1973–
    The story of the boxer / by Martha Mulvany.
        p.   cm. — (Dogs throughout history)
    Includes index.
    Summary: Discusses the history of Boxer dogs from the Middle Ages to the present, describing their role as hunters, fighters, and companions, as well as their work for the military in World Wars I and II.
    ISBN 0-8239-5519-2 (lib. bdg.)
    1. Boxer (Dog breed)—History—Juvenile literature. 2. Boxer (Dog breed)—Juvenile literature. [1. Boxer (Dog breed) 2. Dogs.] I. Series.
    SF429.B75M85 1998
    636.73—dc21
                                                                98-49411
                                                                    CIP
                                                                    AC

Manufactured in the United States of America

Contents

All About Boxers

Do Boxers really box? Not exactly, but sometimes they look like they do. Boxers got their name because they strike out with their front paws when they play or fight with other animals. Boxers are known for their square-shaped heads, muscular bodies, and powerful jaws. Their short, glossy **coats** are usually light to medium brown, with black around the **muzzle**. Some Boxers' coats have thin black stripes. Boxers might look stern, but they are friendly and loyal dogs. It is these **qualities**, along with their strength and hard work, that have made Boxers so helpful to people throughout history.

◀ *Boxers are friendly dogs, even if their faces don't always show it.*

Hunting Dogs

The Boxer's **ancestors** lived in Germany as early as the 1100s. At that time, people liked to go with their friends and neighbors to hunt forest animals. These hunters wanted to catch deer, bears, and wild boar. Large dogs, called **Bullenbeissers**, helped people hunt. Bullenbeissers were similar to today's Boxers, but even larger and stronger. The word Bullenbeisser is German for "bull-biter." These dogs had big teeth, and jaws powerful enough to hold on to a strong animal until the hunters arrived to capture it.

Bullenbeissers helped hunters catch forest animals many years ago. ▶

Bull-Biters

In Germany, people also used Bullenbeissers for entertainment. Some Bullenbeissers were trained to do tricks in the circus. More often, Bullenbeissers were trained to fight. In the 1700s, **bullbaiting** and **bearbaiting** were popular activities. Fights were held between Bullenbeissers and bulls or bears. People watched these fights the way people watch sports games today. Often during these terrible fights, the animals would be hurt, or even killed. By the 1800s, people decided animal baiting was cruel. It was finally outlawed by the 1850s.

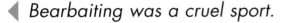 *Bearbaiting was a cruel sport.*

Boxers Helping Butchers

In Germany during the 1800s, people started to **breed** a smaller Boxer relative, which the Germans called the **Boxel**. Boxels were working dogs that usually helped butchers. People bought fresh meat from butchers, who had live pigs and cows. Boxels kept the animals under control. Sometimes a butcher couldn't get hold of an animal. When this happened, he would call out, "Boxel!" The Boxel would come, barking and running, to bite at the animal's nose. Then, the Boxel would push the animal into a stable, where the butcher could catch it.

This Boxer may be a relative of the Boxels that used to help butchers. ▶

A Loyal Friend Called Keeper

Not all Boxers living in the 1800s were working dogs. One famous Boxer was a pet named Keeper. Keeper belonged to Emily Brontë. Emily was a famous British writer, and Keeper was her favorite companion. When she walked out over the foggy **moors**, Keeper always went with her. Emily loved Keeper so much that even when Emily was sick and dying, she took good care of her dog. She got up out of bed, went outside, and gave Keeper the last dinner she would ever feed him. Emily came back inside and soon died. Emily and Keeper were friends for life.

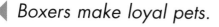
Boxers make loyal pets.

Boxers Are Beautiful

Bullenbeissers and Boxels did not look exactly like the Boxers we know today. They were larger and had different colored coats. In 1895, a German man named George Alt began to breed Boxers so they would all look alike. People already loved Boxers because they were smart and strong. George wanted his Boxers to be beautiful too. When breeding them, George chose Boxers that had certain physical qualities, like brown fur with black faces. He bred them so their babies had those qualities, too. George helped to make the Boxer the handsome dog it is today.

These Boxer puppies get their cute looks from their parents. ▶

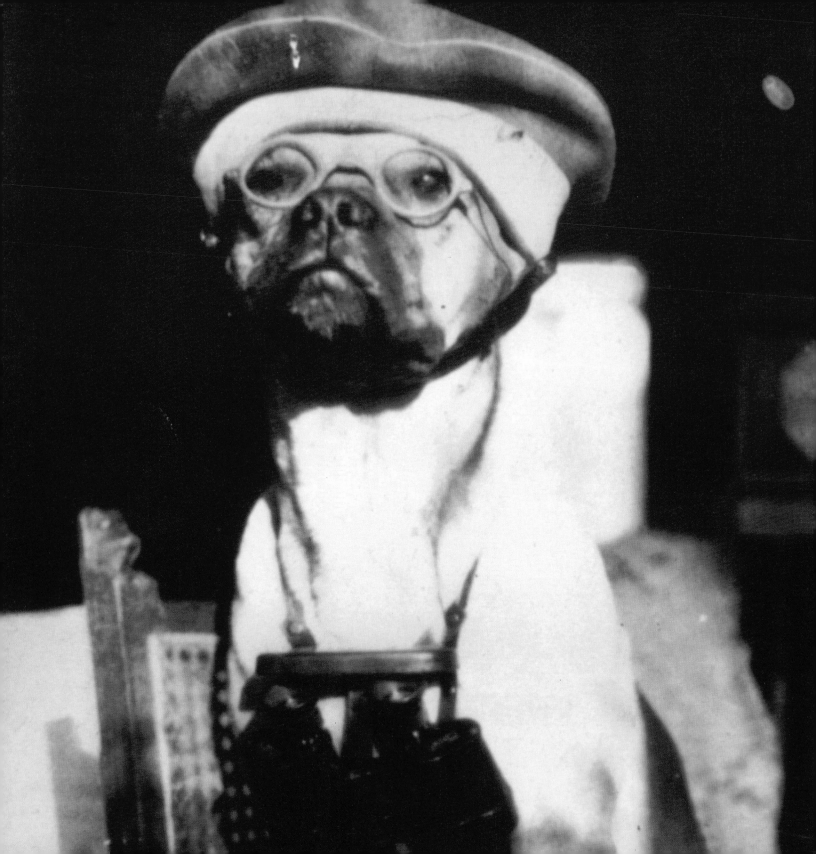

Boxers in World War I

During World War I, from 1914 to 1918, the German army had many jobs for Boxers. The dogs had to be brave, smart, and strong. Boxers were **courier** dogs, taking messages through dangerous areas. They also found **snipers**. If an enemy was shooting at the Germans, a Boxer would be sent to locate him by following his scent. One famous Boxer working for the army was named Rolf von Vogelsberg. Rolf found and cornered whole groups of snipers by himself. He was so fierce that his biting and snarling kept enemies where he found them until German soldiers arrived.

◄ *A soldier dressed this Boxer in his hat, glasses, and binoculars during World War I.*

Boxers in World War II

After World War I, Germany was a very poor country. Food had to be **rationed**. The Germans knew that another war might start soon. Only dogs who could be helpful to the army were given food. Since Boxers had done such a good job in World War I, they were fed. When World War II began in 1939, the Germans had work for Boxers again. Boxers carried messages, protected soldiers, and guarded prisons. Other countries like England used Boxers in the war, too. They were courageous and loyal dogs. Unfortunately, many Boxers were killed in the fighting.

This Boxer was a good friend to these brave British soldiers who fought in World War II. ▶

18

Brave Boxers

Boxers are very brave dogs. They have served in wars and protected people's homes. Boxers make excellent guard dogs because they have a good sense of smell and great hearing. Boxers are strong, so they are able to protect their owners.

In 1990, Mo, a Boxer that lives in Utah, saved two-year-old Lacy Merrifield from an attack by another dog. Lacy was playing in her grandparents' yard when a huge dog knocked her over. Mo ran to the rescue! Growling and barking, he pushed the other dog off their property. Mo's bravery saved little Lacy!

Boxers are not only great helpers, they make good friends, too.

Boxers Today

   Throughout their history, Boxers have been very important to people. Hunting, helping butchers, working in war, protecting children, and guarding homes, the Boxer has always been a dependable dog. While Boxers are excellent workers, they are also fun and friendly. Today, the Boxer's most important job is being a family pet. Boxers love to be around people, and they're great with kids. Just like a kid, the Boxer is always ready to run and play. It is their playful spirit, good nature, and loyalty that make Boxers such wonderful companions.

Web Sites:

http://www.mindspring.com/~eetee/home.html
http://www.akc.org/clubs/abc/abc-home.htm

Glossary

ancestor (AN-ses-ter) A relative who lived long ago.

bearbaiting (BAYR-bay-ting) When people force a bear to fight with another animal.

Boxel (BOK-sul) An early relative of the Boxer who helped butchers.

breed (BREED) When people bring a male and female animal together so that they will have babies.

bullbaiting (BUL-bay-ting) When people force a bull to fight with another animal.

Bullenbeisser (BUL-in-BY-zur) A relative of the Boxer that is now extinct.

coat (COHT) An animal's fur.

courier (KUR-ee-ur) Someone who carries messages.

moor (MOOR) A damp, grassy field, usually in Great Britain.

muzzle (MUH-zul) The jaws and nose of an animal.

quality (KWA-lih-tee) A feature that makes an individual special.

rationed (RA-shund) When food and products are given to people in limited amounts.

sniper (SNY-pur) A person who shoots at an enemy from a hidden place.

Index